Genre Realistic Fiction

Essential Question
How can we reuse what we already have?

The Great Book Swap

by Alan Mitchell • illustrated by Susan Lexa-Senning

Chapter 1
Too Many Books

"Mario, how is the cleanup going?" asks Mario's mother. "You know your room in the new house is smaller. You can't take all of your things."

"I have so many books, Mama," says Mario. "How do I decide which ones to keep?"

"Choose your favorites," his mother tells him.

Mario gazes at his bookcase, which is overflowing with books. He feels discouraged. He wants to keep all of his books.

Mario picks up a book about vets. "This one isn't mine," says Mario.

"That was Selina's book. She decided to become a vet after reading it," says his mother.

Please return this book to: Selina Ruiz

The Story of a Vet

Then Mario's mother hands him a book and says, "I think this one is yours. It was in the den."

"*Amazing Robot Facts!* That's my favorite book ever." He starts turning the pages. "Wow, I still *really* want a robot car."

Mario's friend Sam, who lives close by, arrives. Mario shows him the book.

Mario says, "Remember when we pretended to be robots all weekend. We wouldn't go to bed..."

"Because robots don't sleep," says Sam.

"In the end Papa read us the Second Law of Robotics. Here it is," says Mario. "Robots must obey the orders given by human beings."

"My little brother would love this book. Are you giving it away?" Sam asks as he and Mario read the robot book.

"No way! It's my favorite book," says Mario.

"Do you read your books more than once?" asks Sam.

"Sometimes," says Mario. Then he looks at his books. "I guess I don't really need to read all of these again. It might be good to pass them on to someone else. Then I will have room for more books."

STOP AND CHECK

Why is Mario sorting through his books?

Chapter 2
A Home Without Books

In class, Mario's teacher asks about books they like.

"*Amazing Robot Facts!* is a really good book," says Mario.

Rene gives a snort. "Is it as good as the game *Wrestling Robots*?"

"Rene, why don't you tell us about your favorite book," says the teacher.

"I don't know. I don't have any... I mean, I don't like books," he says. "They're old technology."

Mario wonders if that is really true.

"Hey Mario," says Rene after class. "Why don't you come and play *Wrestling Robots* later."

"Okay," says Mario. "I'll bring the book about robots. We'll see which is better."

At Rene's house, Mario puts the book down while he and Rene play *Wrestling Robots*. Mario notices that there are no books in Rene's room.

When it is time to go, Mario sees that Rene's brother and sister are reading the robot book.

"I've learned everything about robots from this book," says Frankie proudly. He is jubilant.

"Everything?" Rene asks his brother. "Do you know how robots wrestle?"

Frankie doesn't want to close the book. He sighs in frustration when he hands it over to Mario.

"I could lend the book to Frankie," thinks Mario, "but Sam also wanted it. I need to think about what's fair."

STOP AND CHECK

What is Mario's favorite book?

9

By the next day, Mario has a plan. He talks to his teacher.

"Miss Foster, I have some books I don't need. I'm sure others do, too. I have an idea for a book swap. People could donate their old books. They can swap them for other books. We could donate the remaining books to the library."

"Recycling books is a great idea, Mario," says Miss Foster. "I will book the school hall. You make a flyer."

THE GREAT
SCHOOL BOOK SWAP

Mario and Sam draw up a flyer.
Miss Foster has copies printed.

The Great
School Book Swap

Donate your old books and
take new books in return.

This Friday at 1:00 p.m.
in the school hall.

Leftover books to go to the library.

Mario hands one of the flyers to
a frowning Rene.

"No thanks," says Rene. "I told you.
I don't bother with old technology."

Mario remembers his visit to Rene's home. He talks to Miss Foster.

"What if someone has no books to swap? Could they get a book if they help out?"

"Another good idea," says Miss Foster.

Miss Foster asks for volunteers to sort books and help out on the day of the swap.

Mario puts up his hand to volunteer. He is pleased to see that Rene also has his hand up.

STOP AND CHECK

What is a book swap?

Chapter 4
Books for All

The day of the book swap arrives. The school hall is full of tables of books. Students are picking up books and talking about them. A girl picks up *The Story of a Vet.*

Mario says, "That was my sister's book. She is studying to be a vet now."

"I can't wait to read it," says the girl.

Rene is in charge of a table of books. He calls Mario and Sam over. He is proud of the display he has made.

"You might like this one," says Rene. He picks a book out from the bottom of a pile.

"Thanks, I haven't read it," says Mario, taking the book.

Rene checks the book off the book list. Mario looks at the list. He sees there is a check next to *Amazing Robot Facts!*

Rene looks a little embarrassed.

Mario says, "Did you choose that book for Frankie?"

"Yes...for Frankie," says Rene, smiling. "That kid just doesn't understand that books are old technology."

STOP AND CHECK

Why did Rene look embarrassed?

Respond to Reading

Summarize

Use details from the story to summarize *The Great Book Swap*. Your chart may help you.

Details

↓

Point of View

Text Evidence

1. How can you tell that this story is realistic fiction? Genre

2. Does Mario believe Rene when he says he doesn't like books? Look at page 7 for clues. Point of View

3. Find the homograph *close* on page 9. What clues in the sentence help you figure out its meaning? Homographs

4. Use details from the story to write about Mario and the feelings he has towards his books. How do these feelings change? Write about Reading

Compare Texts
Read about how to organize a book and toy swap.

Why Not Swap?

Do you enjoy the toys and books at your friend's house? It's fun to have something different to play with or read. That's part of the excitement of getting new things. Even so, sometimes your shiny new toy ends up in a pile on the closet floor, or your favorite new book gathers dust on your bookshelf.

Why not recycle your books and toys? This is a form of conservation. Resources such as trees are used to make books. If we reuse books, some trees are saved for future use.

You can recycle by holding a book and toy swap. Gather up books and toys that you no longer want. Ask your friends to do the same.

Make some tickets for your swap. Give everyone a ticket for each item they donate. Then everyone can trade a ticket for a new toy or book.

Donate any leftover toys or books to a library or hospital.

When we recycle books we save trees for future use.

Make a Bookmark

You Need

- envelope
- scissors
- glue
- magazine pages

What to Do

1. Cut a triangle from the corner of an envelope.

2. Cut out a magazine picture that is the same size as the envelope corner.

3. Glue the picture to one side of the triangle. You might need to tinker to get everything lined up.

4. Slide the triangle bookmark over the corner of a page.

Make Connections

Think of another way to reuse something that you already have. Essential Question

Why is it important to reuse what you have? Use what you learned from *The Great Book Swap* and *Why Not Swap?* to support your response. Text to Text

Focus on

Genre

Realistic Fiction Realistic fiction stories are often set in the present. The characters are like real people. The things that happen are things that happen to real people.

Read and Find *The Great Book Swap* is set in the present, and the characters are realistic. The things that happen in the story are things that could happen in real life.

Your Turn

Imagine that you are moving to a new house. You can only keep some of your things. Write about what you would do to reuse or recycle the other items. Make the story as realistic as possible.